WHEN THE LAST
A C O R N
IS FOUND

BY DEBORAH LATZKE

ACKNOWLEDGEMENTS

Dedicated to the "goodfinder" in each of us in the hope that we find the power of love within and share it with a world that eagerly awaits the treasured gift of who we are and why we came to be.

With heartfelt gratitude to each participant of the "Acorn Project" for sharing your gift. May the seeds of love, passion and commitment that you have planted in bringing this project to life touch the lives of others as deeply as they have touched mine.

WITH SPECIAL THANKS

JOYCE ECKES ... SEEDS OF SUPPORT

PEGGY LAURITSEN ... SEEDS OF DESIGN

JACKIE LEVIN ... SEEDS OF VISION

PAM SCHOFFNER ... SEEDS OF EDITING

CHERYL VOLKMAN ... SEEDS OF WISDOM

IDEAL PRINTERS ... SEEDS OF REALITY

When the Last Acorn is Found
©1993 Deborah Latzke
P.O. Box 50656
Minneapolis, Minnesota 55405-0656
PRINTED ON RECYCLED PAPER

"A GOOD FINDER IS ONE
WHO LOOKS FOR AND FINDS
WHAT IS GOOD IN HIM OR
HERSELF, IN OTHERS, AND
IN ALL SITUATIONS OF LIFE.
IT IS PROBABLY TRUE THAT
WE USUALLY DO FIND WHAT
WE ARE LOOKING FOR."

JOHN POWELL

DEEP WITHIN A FOREST STANDS AN ANCIENT AND
MAGNIFICENT OAK TREE.

THOSE WHO HAVE FOUND IT SAY IT IS ENCHANTED
WITH THE SECRET OF LIFE. THEY BELIEVE THE TREE WILL
WAIT ETERNALLY FOR EACH OF US TO DISCOVER
AND REALIZE ITS POWERS.

VERY FEW KNOW HOW OR WHY THE INCREDIBLE TREE
CHANGED THEIR LIVES. THEY ONLY KNOW
THAT IT DID AND ARE FOREVER GRATEFUL.

ALL WHO HAVE VISITED THE OAK TELL OF REMARKABLY SIMILAR EXPERIENCES. UPON ENTERING THE FOREST, THEY WERE DRAWN TO A PATH LEADING THEM TO THE TREE. WHILE STANDING BENEATH ITS CANOPY OF COLOR, A SINGLE ACORN DROPPED TO THEIR FEET. AS EACH VISITOR BENT DOWN TO PICK UP THE ACORN, A WAVE OF LOVE WASHED OVER THEIR ENTIRE BEING AND SETTLED DEEP WITHIN THEIR HEART. THEY PEACEFULLY TURNED TO FOLLOW THE PATH HOMEWARD, BUT TO LIVE LIFE DIFFERENTLY.

FROM THAT DAY FORWARD, MANY HAVE CARRIED THEIR
ACORNS WITH THEM IN THEIR POCKETS OR IN POUCHES
TIED AROUND THEIR NECKS THAT RESTED OVER THEIR
HEARTS. EACH TIME THEY TOUCH THE ACORN, THEY
REMEMBER THE POWERFUL LOVE THEY CARRY WITHIN
AND RENEW THEIR VOW TO TEACH AND LEARN
FROM THAT PLACE OF LOVE.

FOR THOSE WHO BELIEVE, THE ACORN IS AN
EVER-PRESENT REMINDER OF WHO THEY ARE AND
WHY THEY CAME TO BE.

SOME RETURN TO THE FOREST SEEKING AN EXPLANATION
FOR THEIR TRANSFORMATION AND FIND THE ONLY CLUES
IN A LEGEND TOLD BY THE WISE, OLD WOMAN WHO LIVES
NEAR THE FOREST'S EDGE. EACH TIME SHE IS ASKED TO
TELL THE STORY, SHE REMOVES AN ACORN FROM HER
POCKET, FOLDS IT GENTLY IN THE PALM OF HER HAND
AND BEGINS . . .

"SOME WILL BELIEVE WHAT I TELL YOU IS FACT AND SOME WILL BELIEVE IT IS FICTION.

It is up to you to decide what you believe, and what you believe will become your truth.

THE ANCIENT OAK TREE IS INHABITED BY TINY MEN,
WOMEN AND CHILDREN WHO CALL THEMSELVES THE
ACORN PEOPLE. THEIR HOME IN THE TREE IS A MAGICAL
AND MARVELOUS PLACE TO BE . . .

EACH BABY BORN INTO THE ACORN COMMUNITY IS
DELIVERED WITH A SIMPLE, THREE-WORD INSTRUCTION:
TEACH ONLY LOVE. EVERY ACORN PARENT FOR
GENERATIONS HAS FOLLOWED THIS INSTRUCTION.

THE ACORNS LOVE WITHOUT QUESTION OR CONDITION.
FOR THEM, LOVING COMES AS EASILY AND NATURALLY
AS BREATHING.

THE ACORNS MAKE A CONSCIOUS EFFORT TO LIVE IN THE PRESENT MOMENT. EVERYONE AGE 5 TO 65 WEARS A WATCH. BUT INSTEAD OF MARKING TIME WITH MINUTES AND HOURS, THEIR TIMEKEEPERS MERELY FLASH A SINGLE, IRIDESCENT WORD: NOW. THE YOUNGEST AND OLDEST ACORNS HAVE NO NEED TO WEAR WATCHES, FOR THEY NEVER SEEM TO FORGET . . . "NOW" IS WHAT TRULY MATTERS.

EACH AND EVERY ACORN IS BORN WITH A SPECIAL GIFT, A TALENT WHICH IS RECOGNIZED, NURTURED AND CELEBRATED. EVEN THE YOUNGEST ACORNS SHARE THEIR GIFT BY TEACHING THEIR ELDERS A RENEWED APPRECIATION OF FUN, WONDER AND ADVENTURE.

EVERYONE CONTRIBUTES AND EVERYONE IS
ACKNOWLEDGED FOR THEIR CONTRIBUTION.

THE ACORNS ARE GENERALLY HEALTHY IN BODY, MIND AND SPIRIT. BUT WHEN PAIN OCCURS, THE ACORN REMEDY IS THE SIMPLE HEALING POWER OF LOVE. EVEN THE DEEPEST PAIN DISAPPEARS WITH A TOUCH THAT IS WARM AND GENTLE, WORDS THAT ARE KIND AND COMPASSIONATE, A LOOK THAT IS TENDER AND UNDERSTANDING AND AN ACT THAT IS GENEROUS AND SUPPORTIVE.

THE WISE ACORN PEOPLE ATTRIBUTE THEIR WISDOM TO
THE BELIEF THAT EVERYONE, IN THEIR OWN WAY AND
IN THEIR OWN TIME, CAN AND WILL LEARN WHAT IS
NEEDED TO LIVE A REWARDING AND MEANINGFUL LIFE.
FROM THE TIME THEY ARE VERY YOUNG, THE ACORNS ARE
TAUGHT THE KEYS TO SUCCESS . . .

LOVE YOURSELF . . .
FOR IT MAKES ALL THINGS POSSIBLE

LOVE OTHERS . . . AND YOU WILL LEARN TO GIVE

ALLOW OTHERS TO LOVE YOU . . .
AND YOU WILL LEARN TO RECEIVE

BELIEVE IN YOURSELF . . .
FOR WHAT YOU TRULY BELIEVE, YOU WILL ACHIEVE

MAKE FUN AND LAUGHTER A PRIORITY . . .
LIFE IS TO BE ENJOYED

SEEK OUT OPPORTUNITIES AND POSSIBILITIES . . .
LIFE IS AN ADVENTURE

TAKE RISKS AND FACE FEARS . . .
WONDERFUL THINGS AWAIT YOU IN THE UNKNOWN

MAKE CHOICES WISELY AND WITH LOVE . . .
THE QUALITY OF YOUR LIFE DEPENDS ON IT

SHARE THE GIFT OF WHO YOU ARE . . .
IT'S WHY YOU CAME TO BE

LOVING, BEING LOVED, FEELING CONFIDENT AND CAPABLE,
AND LIVING IN THE POWERFUL TIME OF NOW ALLOWS THE
ACORN PEOPLE TO LIVE IN A STATE OF TOTAL TRUST.
THERE IS NO NEED TO FEAR, JUDGE, CONTROL, DECEIVE OR
MANIPULATE. THE ACORN PEOPLE KNOW THE TRUE
MEANING OF LOVING, HONORING AND RESPECTING
EVERYONE AND EVERYTHING. THEY ESPECIALLY LOVE
THEMSELVES FOR THEY KNOW THEY CAN'T GIVE AWAY TO
OTHERS WHAT THEY HAVE NOT FOUND WITHIN.

THE LIFETIME OF EACH ACORN PERSON INCLUDES ONE
SACRED JOURNEY, SOMETIMES TO A FAR CORNER OF THE
WORLD AND BACK. THEIR MISSION IS TO FIND A SPECIAL
PLACE THAT HAS RICH, DARK SOIL AND IS WARMED BY THE
SUNLIGHT. UPON REACHING THAT DESTINATION, EACH
PLANTS A SINGLE ACORN FROM THE POWERFUL AND
BELOVED TREE. THE WONDROUS SEEDS CONTAIN
THE SECRET TO LIFE . . .

THE ACORN PEOPLE ARE COMMITTED TO PLANTING
THESE SEEDS OF LOVE; IT IS THEIR LEGACY. THEY BELIEVE
THAT WHEN ENOUGH OF THE ACORNS HAVE BEEN FOUND
— NO ONE KNOWS HOW MANY IT WILL TAKE — THE SECRET
OF LIFE WILL BE REVEALED TO ALL AND LOVE WILL RADIATE
FROM THE HEART OF EVERY LIVING BEING."

As the old woman finishes her story, a knowing twinkle shines from her deep brown eyes and she gently returns the acorn to her pocket. Many who hear the story try to question her further. She merely waves her hand, turns and walks slowly back into the forest. Those who listen carefully hear her whisper: "All answers are found within."

PERHAPS YOU'VE ALREADY FOUND YOUR ACORN,

OR MAYBE YOU'LL FIND THE NEXT ONE.

IT WON'T BE LONG NOW.

SOON, VERY SOON,

THE LAST ACORN WILL BE FOUND.

the beginning

The story of the Acorn People started with a single thought which, like a seed, was planted and grew to have a life of its own. The thought became an action, the action became a story, and the story became a book.

When the Last Acorn is Found was inspired by this thought: without exception, we each make a difference. In learning to make positive choices that are wise and loving, we create positive changes that are powerful and lasting. The impact of those choices and changes is felt, not only in our own lives, but within our families, our communities and the world in which we live.

This thought became the theme for several Legacy of Love workshops. At the end of each workshop, a basket of acorns was passed around to the participants. The acorns were intended to be tangible reminders that each day of our lives presents us with the opportunity to plant the seeds of who we are; powerful beings whose presence matters and makes a difference . . . whose possibilities for growth and positive impact are unlimited.

Giving each participant an acorn seemed, at first, to be merely a nice idea. But one day, a woman approached me after the workshop, removed the acorn from her pocket and shared why receiving it was so important and timely in her life. It was then that I realized the power of having an ever-present reminder of our worth and impact.

The story about the wise and loving Acorn People soon followed. I hope you have enjoyed reading it and will share it with others as a tangible reminder of their worth, their power and their potential for creating a brighter, more loving future.

With warm regards,
Deborah Latzke

If you would like to order additional copies, or if you would like information about the Legacy of Love workshops and seminars, please call or write to us.
Legacy of Love , P.O. Box 50656, Minneapolis, MN 55405-0656.
Call Monday through Friday, (612)872-7681
between 9am & 5pm Central Standard Time.

BOOKS BY DEBORAH LATZKE

WHEN THE LAST ACORN IS FOUND

SEARCHING FOR THE ACORN